ORANGUTANS BUILD TREE NESTS

BY ELIZABETH RAUM ILLUSTRATED BY ROMINA MARTÍ

AMICUS ILLUSTRATED and AMICUS INK are published by Amicus
P.O. Box 1329, Mankato, MN 56002
www.amicuspublishing.us

LIBRARY OF CONGRESS CATALOGING-IN-PUBLICATION DATA
Names: Raum, Elizabeth, author. | Martí, Romina, illustrator.
Title: Orangutans build tree nests / by Elizabeth Raum ; illustrated by Romina Martí.
Description: Mankato, Minnesota : Amicus/Amicus Ink, [2018] | Series: Animal builders | Series: Amicus illustrated | Audience: Grade K-3.
Identifiers: LCCN 2016050067 (print) | LCCN 2017003871 (ebook) | ISBN 9781681511726 (library binding) | ISBN 9781681521534 (paperback) | ISBN 9781681512624 (e-book)
Subjects: LCSH: Orangutans—Juvenile literature.
Classification: LCC QL737.P94 R38 2018 (print) | LCC QL737.P94 (ebook) | DDC 599.88/3—dc23
LC record available at https://lccn.loc.gov/2016050067

EDITOR: Rebecca Glaser
DESIGNER: Kathleen Petelinsek

Printed in the United States of America
HC 10 9 8 7 6 5 4 3 2 1
PB 10 9 8 7 6 5 4 3 2 1

ABOUT THE AUTHOR

As a child, Elizabeth Raum hiked through the Vermont woods searching for signs that animals lived nearby. She read every animal book in the school library. She now lives in North Dakota and writes books for young readers. Many of her books are about animals. To learn more, go to: elizabethraum.net

ABOUT THE ILLUSTRATOR

Romina Martí is an illustrator who lives and works in Barcelona, Spain, where her ideas come to life for all audiences. She loves to discover and draw all kinds of creatures from around the planet, who then become the main characters for the majority of her work. To learn more, go to: rominamarti.com

On two faraway islands in Asia, orangutans swing through their rainforest habitat. Mama Orangutan teaches baby how to find food. When they grow tired . . .

. . . Mama looks for a place to sleep. Orangutans are solitary. They usually live alone. But babies stay with their mothers for several years.

For an afternoon nap, Mama builds a quick nest. But now it's late. Every night, she builds a new, strong nest for a good night's sleep.

The first step is to find the right tree. Not this one! There's no peace and quiet in a fruit tree. Noisy fruit bats eat all night. Other hungry animals may stop for a late night snack or an early breakfast.

This one works! It has a thick trunk and strong branches. The leaves provide shade. They help keep rain away. Mama chooses a sturdy branch or group of branches to hold her nest.

Baby watches as Mama builds. Mama stands on a branch and bends big branches toward the center. The branches snap, but they don't break.

They form the base of the nest. It must be very strong. Orangutans are heavy. They weigh as much as a grown-up human.

Mama adds small leafy branches to the base. She braids the tips together. They form a mattress. The nest is strongest at the edges. The middle is soft and bouncy. Mama works fast. Building a nest takes about 15 minutes.

Finally, Mama adds special touches. She piles small leafy twigs at one end. These are pillows.

She makes a blanket of leafy branches.
If it rains, she uses a big leaf for an umbrella.

Mama and her baby are high in the canopy, the leafy world at the top of the rainforest.

Tigers roam the forest below. So do clouded leopards and human hunters. But Mama and baby are safe, sleeping high in their nest.

After a good night's sleep, Mama Orangutan and baby wake up. They swing through the trees in search of tasty fruit.

Later, baby takes apart an old nest to learn how they are built. He tries to build his own nest, but it's a mess. He needs years of practice! He'll sleep in Mama's nest for now.

Where Orangutans Live

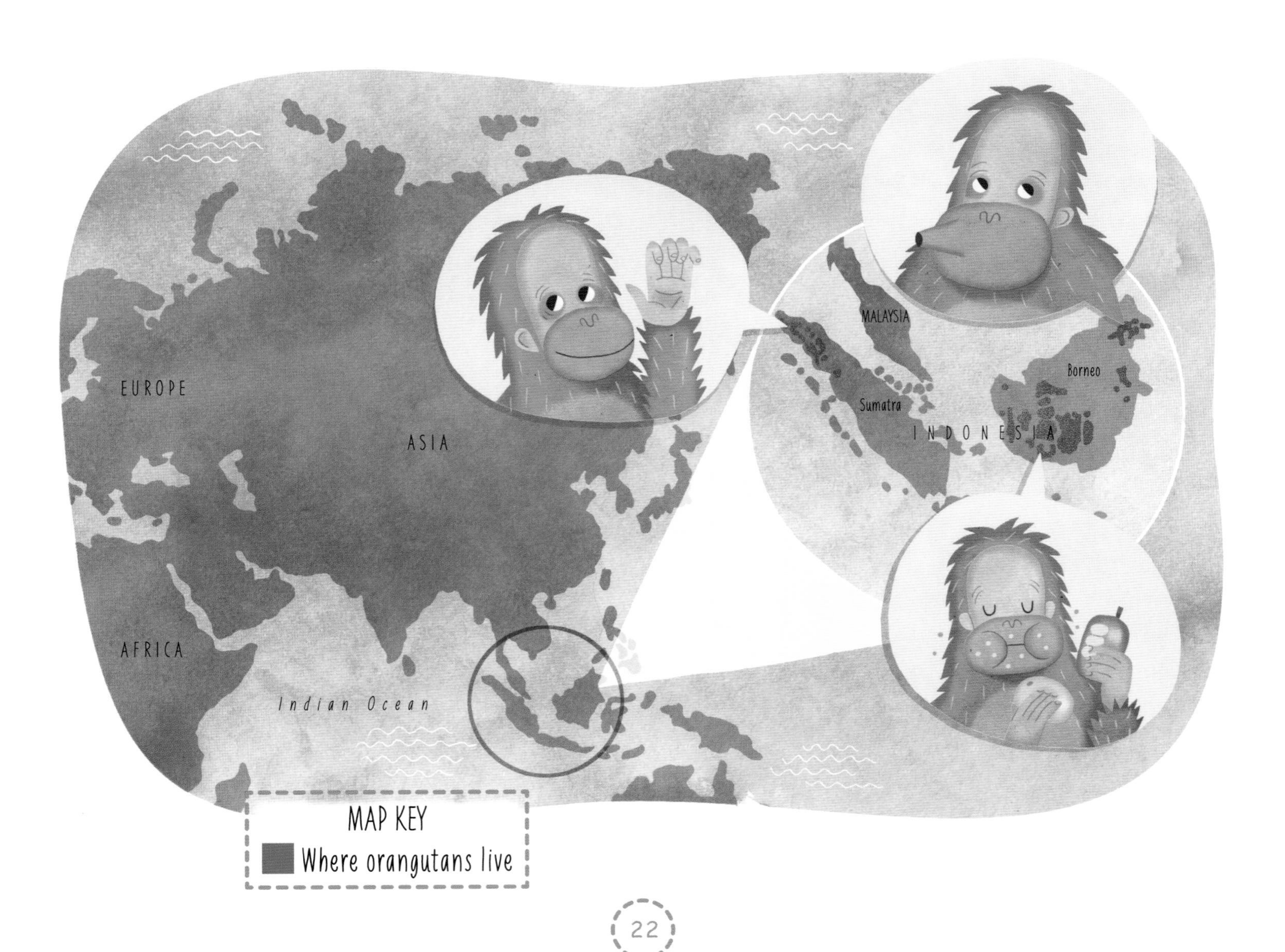

Build Like an Orangutan

Orangutans build nests by bending and weaving tree branches. Try this method using cardboard and paper strips to build a model nest.

WHAT ORANGUTANS USE	WHAT YOU NEED
Strong tree branches	A sturdy paper plate, about 7 inches (18 cm) across Thin cardboard strips, about 1 x 8 inches (2.5 cm x 20 cm)
Smaller tree branches	Strips of paper, about ½ inch by 7 inches (1.2 cm x 20 cm)

WHAT YOU DO

1. Cut a circle out of the middle of the paper plate.
2. Cut a cereal box into four strips, each about 1 inch (2.5 cm) wide and 8 inches (20 cm) long.
3. Fold the cardboard strips over the lip of the paper plate. Space them equally apart and then staple them down. (The cardboard should cover the hole in the plate.)
4. Lay five or six thin paper strips over the cardboard strips. Staple them to the edge. Now weave more strips through them to make a mattress.
5. Place a small stuffed animal on the nest while holding the nest in the air. Does it hold your animal? If not, how could you weave it to be stronger?

GLOSSARY

canopy The cover formed by the upper leafy branches in a forest.

clouded leopard A wild cat with cloud-shaped spots on its fur that lives on the islands of Borneo and Sumatra.

habitat The place where a person or animal usually lives.

orangutan A large, long-armed ape that lives on the islands of Borneo and Sumatra.

rainforest A tropical forest with tall, broad-leaved trees in an area of high rainfall.

solitary Living alone, not in families or groups.

READ MORE

Hibbert, Clare. ***Orangutan Orphans***. New York: PowerKids Press, 2015.

Leaf, Christina. ***Baby Orangutans***. Minneapolis: Bellwether Media, 2015.

Morey, Allan. ***Orangutans Are Awesome!*** North Mankato, Minn.: Capstone Press, 2016.

Sabatino, Michael. ***Being An Orangutan***. New York: Gareth Stevens, 2014.

WEBSITES

Orangutan: National Geographic Kids

http://kids.nationalgeographic.com/animals/orangutan

See photos of orangutans and read about their life in the trees.

Orangutans: San Diego Zoo Kids

http://kids.sandiegozoo.org/animals/mammals/orangutan

Watch videos of orangutans, listen to them, and learn more about them.

Ranger Rick "Orangutans"

https://www.nwf.org/Kids/Ranger-Rick/Animals/Mammals/Orangutans.aspx

Read an article from Ranger Rick magazine about orangutans.

Every effort has been made to ensure that these websites are appropriate for children. However, because of the nature of the Internet, it is impossible to guarantee that these sites will remain active indefinitely or that their contents will not be altered.